SUGAR ART
Ideas

SWEETS & TREATS

SUGAR ART
Ideas

SWEETS & TREATS

LINDSAY JOHN BRADSHAW

Series Editor: ALISON LEACH

SELECT
EDITIONS

Published 1992 by The Promotional Reprint Co Ltd,
Exclusively for Selecta Book Ltd,
Devizes UK and the Book Company,
Sydney in Australia

ISBN 1 85648 075 5

Printed and bound in Hong Kong through Bookbuilders Ltd

ACKNOWLEDGEMENTS
The Publishers would like to thank the following for their help and advice:
Julia Catchpole of C.E.P. Chocolate & Sugar Moulds, 7 Durrington Road,
Bournemouth BH7 6PU
B. R. Mathews & Son, 12 Gipsy Hill, Upper Norwood, London SE19 1NN
David Mellor, 26 James Street, Covent Garden, London WC2E 8PA
Keylink Limited, Blackburn Road, Rotherham S61 2DR
Wheatsheaf Graphics, 50 Grays Inn Road, London WC1X 8LT

Warning
Cocktail sticks and wired flowers must only be used for display purposes in sugarcraft. Great care
should always be taken to ensure there is no possibility of any particles being eaten accidentally.

Important: use only one set of measurements. The quantities given in metric are not always exact conversions of the imperial measurements. Cup conversions of imperial measurements are given below.

Imperial	Cups
5 fl oz liquid	$\frac{2}{3}$ cup
10 fl oz liquid	$1\frac{1}{4}$ cups
20 fl oz liquid	$2\frac{1}{2}$ cups
40 fl oz liquid	5 cups
1 lb granulated or caster (superfine) sugar	2 cups
1 lb brown sugar	2 cups
1 lb icing (confectioner's) sugar	$3\frac{1}{2}$ cups
1 lb butter	2 cups
1 lb dried fruit	3 cups
1 lb flour	4 cups
8 oz glacé cherries	1 cup
4 oz chopped nuts	1 cup
4 oz cocoa powder	1 cup
1 oz flour	$\frac{1}{4}$ cup
1 oz granulated or caster (superfine) sugar	2 tablespoons
1 oz butter	2 tablespoons

CONTENTS

FOREWORD

I feel privileged to have been asked to write the foreword for SWEETS AND TREATS, the latest book by Lindsay John Bradshaw.

This book is unique since it not only gives the decorator superb instructions on how to make the sweets and chocolates but it also places special emphasis on the decoration and presentation of these goods. Lindsay leaves nothing out and his book covers all aspects of this delightful art. It is so attractively presented that everyone who reads it will wish to go ahead and follow the ideas.

I am sure that one of the main attractions will be that this book is the work of one of our country's top craftsmen, of whom we can be proud. I have known Lindsay since he started teaching some eight years ago and have always admired both his brilliant artistic skills and his natural ability when teaching and demonstrating to challenge and inspire the novice and advanced student alike.

As well as being a Lecturer in Cake Design and Decoration at the Salford College of Technology, Lindsay has recently been appointed Editor of *British Sugarcraft News*: his many skills and hard work in this capacity are very much admired and appreciated.

I know that this book will fill a void in the literature on sugarcraft. I wish Lindsay the success with it that he well deserves.

June E. Elwood, M.Inst.B.B., M.C.F.A.(C.G.)
Principal, The June Elwood Cake Artistry Studio, Manchester
Founder member, The British Sugarcraft Guild

INTRODUCTION

With sugar art becoming more and more popular, the need for new ideas has increased equally. In this series each book covers a specialized area of cake or confectionery decoration, combining numerous original ideas with a few old favourites executed with a new approach.

The emphasis throughout is on design and decoration, offering the discerning cake decorator a range of colourful and attractively decorated sweets and treats.

Many of the sugarcraft techniques will probably already be familiar to you, making sweets and treats an easy extension from your existing cake decorating interests – one that may even take over from your royal icing or sugarpaste work!

Flavour and texture are all important in sweets and treats, so it is essential not to substitute cheaper ingredients. The recipes developed especially for this book do not skimp on quality in any way. The combination of the best available ingredients, professional production techniques and imaginative decoration, both classic and modern, will enable you to achieve results of a very high standard.

Many of the recipes require the minimum amount of equipment, although some call for more specialized items to give a more professional finish.

I hope you will enjoy making the sweets and treats described in this book. Don't eat too many while you are preparing them – save some for your friends so that they too can experience both the delicious flavourings and your artistic skills!

Lindsay John Bradshaw

INGREDIENTS

Most of the tools and equipment used for making sweets and treats are ordinary kitchen or household items. The more unusual items are available from cake decorating shops and specialist sugarcraft suppliers.

Choice of ingredients

To make delicious sweets and treats good quality ingredients are essential. When choosing ingredients from nuts and dried fruits to chocolate and liqueurs, always buy the best available. It is much better to pay a little bit more so that the end products taste really good.

Chocolate

The two main types of chocolate used in sugarcraft are baker's chocolate and couverture.

Baker's chocolate is sometimes referred to as a covering. As it does not require any special preparation, it is far easier to work with than couverture. Baker's chocolate does not have as good a flavour as its far superior counterpart. Couverture is often called 'the real thing' because of its excellent flavour and smoothness. It is more expensive and needs tempering before it can be used.

All the recipes in this book requiring chocolate can be made with either baker's or couverture – the choice is yours – but for really special items like the truffles and chocolate liqueurs, the extra cost of using couverture is justified as it marries well with the flavourings and spirits used in the recipes.

Baker's chocolate is available from all sugarcraft suppliers and most large supermarkets. It can be bought in slabs or in the form of buttons. The main difference from couverture is that most of the cocoa butter has been removed and been replaced with a vegetable fat, eliminating the need for tempering and also producing a softer-cutting set.

Use a double jacketed saucepan to melt the chocolate over hot but not boiling water. Heat to 38–43°C (100–110°F) or until smooth with no lumps. Take care not to overheat the chocolate (particularly important if not using a thermometer) as otherwise fat bloom (white streaks) may appear. Never allow steam to get into the chocolate. Baker's chocolate can be refrigerated to quicken the contraction if using moulds.

Sweets made with couverture will have a far superior gloss, more smoothness to the palate and an outstandingly better flavour. You can purchase couverture from specialist sugarcraft suppliers and bakery sundriesmen. Do not substitute bars of dessert chocolate as these are not pure couverture.

Tempering the chocolate involves heating and then cooling it to various specified temperatures so that the cocoa butter crystallizes to produce a high gloss and good 'snap' when set. A sugar thermometer is essential for accuracy.

Chop the chocolate into small pieces and place in a double jacketed saucepan over simmering, *not* boiling water. When the chocolate reaches 46°C (115°F), remove the pan from the jacket and heat and place in a bowl or sink of cold water. Stir the chocolate until it cools to 27–28°C (80–82°F). Return the pan to the jacket and heat to 31°C (88°F). The chocolate is now tempered and ready for use.

For tempering milk chocolate the temperatures should be 1°C (2°F) lower at *all* stages.

The procedure for tempering white couverture is similar but refer to the manufacturers' specifications for recommended temperatures.

Incorrectly tempered couverture will not set as it should and it will be difficult to release the chocolate from the moulds. White or grey bloom may also be visible.

Ganache

Several of the recipes in this book refer to a ganache base. Ganache is a rich cream and chocolate mixture which can be piped, spread, poured or moulded. It is a most versatile medium and well worth making for its flavour and smoothness. Milk, plain or white chocolate can be used and the ganache can be flavoured to make numerous delicious variations.

Flavourings

Most of the flavourings mentioned in this book are the real products. If you replace these with essences, you will reduce the cost considerably but equally you will reduce the quality of the flavourings. The main flavourings used in the book are rum, brandy, kirsch, maraschino and such liqueurs as Grand Marnier and Tia Maria. The only essences used are vanilla and almond.

Fillings

All the fillings demand quality, freshness and good flavour. Use butter and double (thick) dairy cream where stated. Fresh nuts and fruits are readily available at supermarkets, where many different varieties are prepacked.

MOULDS

A moulded chocolate shell is the basis of many of the sweets and treats in this book. To avoid repeating the procedure in each recipe, the details are fully explained here, with cross-references where necessary.

A selection of commercially available chocolate moulds can be purchased from sugarcraft suppliers. Provided you look after the moulds during and after use, they should give you years of service. The flexible, clear plastic type are quite inexpensive while the sturdier and probably more serviceable, brown-coloured plastic moulds can be up to six times more expensive.

Making moulded chocolates

First ensure that your mould is spotless. Use clean cotton wool to polish inside each shape carefully, including all the crevices and corners. This will ensure that you achieve a better gloss on your chocolate work.

Prepare your baker's chocolate or couverture as described above, taking care to adhere to the recommended temperatures and procedures.

Pour or pipe chocolate into the shapes, filling to the top edge. Tap the tray gently to remove any air bubbles, then leave to start setting. Fill a second tray of moulds while the first is setting.

Check the moulds frequently at regular intervals to see if the chocolate is setting around the edges. As soon as it is, turn the tray upside down over your chocolate pan and drain off the excess chocolate.

Use a small palette knife to clean off any remaining chocolate and then place the tray upside down to let the chocolate finish setting. This will make a small rim form around the inside edge which is ideal to work to when sealing the base of the chocolates. If you do not like the idea of a rim on the inside edge, simply leave the tray the other way up to finish setting.

The chocolate cases are now ready for the fillings. They can then be topped with a thin layer of chocolate to seal in the filling. When filled and sealed, the chocolates can be removed from the moulds by a gentle pressure and with the flexible kind by a little turning of the mould – being careful not to break it.

Cleaning

After use wash the moulds in hot water using a mild detergent, rinse well and allow to drain. Dry the moulds with a soft clean cloth. Polish them with cotton wool (do this again when you use the mould next time) and pack between layers of soft tissue paper until required again.

Hand-moulded chocolates

To save the expense of purchasing moulds, some recipes for hand-moulded chocolates are also included in this book. This method of sweet-making can be just as successful as using plastic pre-shaped moulds. Hand-moulding involves rolling and cutting shapes, and forming balls, ovals or fingers from the various pastes and mixtures.

PEPPERMINT ALPHABETS

Ingredients
royal icing
egg white
assorted food colourings
box of peppermint cream
chocolates

1 Prepare some run-icing for the run-out alphabet letters. Place some freshly made royal icing in a small bowl and add a small amount of unbeaten egg white (water can be used, if preferred), mixing thoroughly with a spoon. Do *not* beat the icing. This would create unwanted air bubbles that would spoil the appearance of your run-out work.

Add sufficient egg white to make a thick creamy consistency. When the spoon is lifted up and a ribbon of icing made across the mixture, the icing should find its own level after a count of about ten. Colour the icing as required. You can make the letters all the same colour or each one different, in which case you will need several small greaseproof paper piping bags, each containing a different colour of run-icing.

2 Make a tracing of the letters, either the full alphabet or just those needed for your chosen name or greeting. Place a piece of waxed paper over the tracing and outline the letters in royal icing and a No1 nozzle. For the outlines you can either use the same colour of icing as the one being used to flood-in or a contrasting colour which looks very effective.

After outlining the letters use scissors to cut a small hole at the end of the piping bag containing the run-icing. The hole should not be bigger than the size of a No2 nozzle. Flood-in the letters carefully and neatly, using a paint brush to assist the flow of the icing. Leave to dry in a gentle heat such as under a desk lamp.

When dry, carefully peel off the letters from the waxed paper, taking care not to damage any of them.

3 Using a little royal icing or melted chocolate, attach a run-out letter to each peppermint cream chocolate. If using royal icing, it is a good idea to colour the icing brown; if any should seep out beneath the letters, it will not be quite as noticeable as white icing would.

Arrange the letters in a fancy box to spell out the name or greeting and finish with a ribbon and bow. A full alphabet of letters packed in a gift box is a novel idea for a youngster who will find this way of learning the alphabet both interesting and delicious.

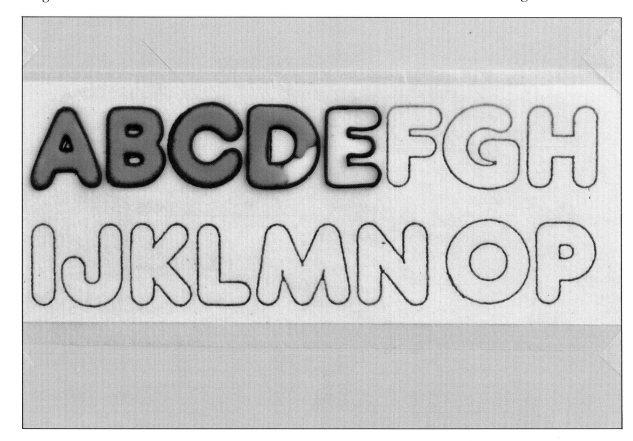

ABCDEF
GHIJKL
MNOPQ
RSTUVW
XYZ 123
4567890

CREAMY FUDGE

Ingredients
125ml (4 fl oz) milk
125ml (4 fl oz) evaporated milk
575g (1¼lb) granulated sugar
125g (4oz) butter
5ml (1 tsp) vanilla essence
melted chocolate for dipping
(*see page 10*)

1 Using a heavy-based saucepan, boil the milk, evaporated milk and sugar. Then add the butter and continue cooking to 115°C (250°F) – soft ball on a sugar thermometer. Stir the mixture occasionally. Remove from the heat and stir in the vanilla essence.

To achieve a grainy-textured fudge, beat the mixture with a wooden spoon until it becomes thick. For a softer texture, let the mixture cool a little before beating.

2 Pour the mixture into a waxed paper-lined baking tray, about 17.5 × 20-cm (7 × 8-in), or into two of the sweet trays described on page 12. Lightly grease the waxed paper with a little butter. Leave the mixture to set for about 12 hours.

Turn the mixture out of the tray in one piece and cut neatly into bite-sized pieces. The fudge can be left as it is or further decorated.

3 The fudge pieces may be dipped in melted milk or plain chocolate either completely or just up to the top edge as shown. Alternatively, you may like to add just a small amount of chocolate decoration in the form of a few lines of spun chocolate as described on page 52.

You can add various nuts, fruits and flavourings to make a selection of different varieties. The quantities given below are for this recipe but you could, for example, easily divide your cooked fudge in two and add half these amounts just before you pour the fudge into the tray to set.

CHOCOLATE FUDGE   Add 30g (2ml) sieved cocoa powder
CHERRY AND WALNUT FUDGE   Add 15ml (1 tbsp) each of chopped glacé cherries and chopped walnuts with a few drops of almond essence to taste
RUM AND RAISIN FUDGE   Add 50g (2oz) raisins which have been soaked in rum for a few hours

GINGER AND HAZELNUT TREATS

Ingredients
225g (8oz) marzipan
5ml 1 tsp) honey
25g (1oz) glacé ginger
25g (1oz) hazelnuts, finely
   chopped and lightly toasted
icing (confectioner's) sugar for
   dusting
melted chocolate for dipping
   (*see page 10*)
pouring fondant
green food colouring

1 Knead the marzipan lightly to make it pliable, warming it slightly if necessary. Add the honey, ginger and hazelnuts and continue mixing until all the ingredients are evenly distributed. Use a little icing sugar to prevent the mixture from sticking to the work surface.

Roll out the mixture, dusting with a little icing sugar, into a long roll about 22-mm ($\frac{7}{8}$-in) diameter.

Cover a cake board with waxed paper. Cut the marzipan; roll into evenly sized pieces about 12-mm ($\frac{1}{2}$-in) thick. Place each piece on the prepared cake board, carefully neatening each one. Leave the pieces for a few hours to become firm before dipping.

2 Prepare the chocolate by melting it gently in a double jacketed pan. Using a dipping fork or metal skewer, pick each piece of marzipan up and submerge in the melted chocolate up to the top edge, lift out and allow any excess chocolate to drain away, smoothing the base of the sweet along the edge of the pan or with a small palette knife. Place the sweets on waxed paper and leave to set.

3 Prepare a small amount of pouring fondant to a relatively firm consistency (not too runny) suitable for piping drops. Use a double jacketed pan to heat the fondant to about 37°C (99°F), adjusting the consistency with water or sugar syrup. Colour the fondant pale green. Place a small amount in a greaseproof paper piping bag and snip off the end with scissors to make an opening about the size of a No2 nozzle. Pipe neat drops of fondant on to each sweet to fill the top surface. Leave to set.

RUM AND RAISIN SNOWBALLS

Ingredients
50g (2oz) raisins
30ml (1 fl oz) rum
225g (8oz) marzipan
green food colouring
royal icing containing glycerine
icing (confectioner's) sugar for
    dusting

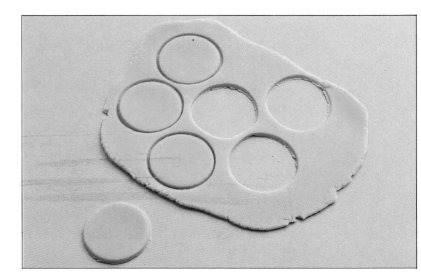

1 Place the raisins in a suitable air-tight plastic container or clean jam jar with screw-topped lid. Pour the rum over the fruit, replace the lid and turn gently to mix. Leave to marinate for about 12 hours, turning the container occasionally.

Colour the marzipan green and roll out, using a little icing sugar for dusting. Cut out small circles of marzipan.

2 Lay a circle of marzipan in the palm of your hand and indent a cupped shape with your thumb.

Place three or four rum-soaked raisins (drain a little if necessary) in the shaped marzipan.

Bring all the edges of the marzipan together gently to form a ball. Lightly roll to retain the ball shape and leave for a few hours to become firm.

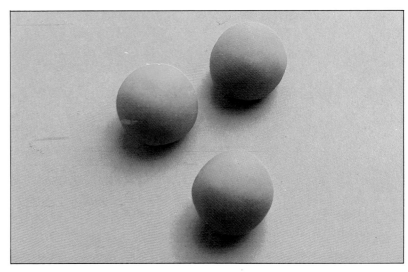

3 Scoop a little royal icing (with glycerine) into the palm of both hands and gently roll each marzipan ball, leaving a peaked surface to resemble snow. Place on waxed paper and leave the icing to firm a little. Lightly re-roll in royal icing again if necessary to cover completely. Place in paper cases ready for presentation.

MARZIPAN CHESTNUTS

Ingredients
marzipan
brown paste food colouring
green paste food colouring
orange paste food colouring
icing (confectioner's) sugar for
   dusting
egg white
royal icing
marzipan varnish

1 Colour half the marzipan dark brown and half dark green using paste food colourings and a little icing sugar to prevent the marzipan sticking to the work surface.

Make the centres of the chestnuts by rolling small balls of the brown-coloured marzipan. Place these on waxed paper and leave for a few hours to become firm. Alternatively, small chocolate truffles could be used for the centres.

2 Roll out the green-coloured marzipan to 3-mm ($\frac{1}{8}$-in) thickness and cut out circles large enough to enclose the chestnut centres. Wrap each chestnut centre in a green-coloured circle enclosing it completely. A little egg white may be required to stick the marzipan but do not use too much or the next step of removing a segment of marzipan may be difficult. Roll with gentle pressure to form neat balls.

Using a small sharp knife cut away a segment as shown and mark the remaining segments using a modelling tool or the back of a small knife.

Pipe on the spikes in royal icing using a No2 nozzle and pulling out to a sharp point.

3 To create the realistic colouring of the nut casings, first tint with pale green colouring and then with orange, avoiding the brown centre portion. Either spray the colour with an airbrush or apply edible petal dust with a dry brush.

Glaze the brown-coloured centres with marzipan varnish.

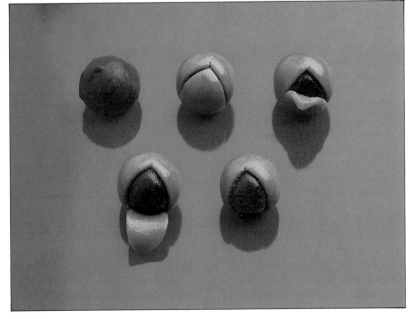

CANDIED PINEAPPLE

Ingredients
225g (8oz) canned pineapple
    rings
175g (6oz) granulated sugar
5ml (1 tsp) lemon juice

1 Drain the juice from the
pineapple rings, setting the
fruit aside. Make up the fruit
juice to 300ml (10 fl oz) with
water and pour into a
saucepan. Add the sugar and
lemon juice and heat until a
syrup is produced. Add the
pineapple rings and bring to
the boil. Remove from the heat
and set aside for 24 hours.

2 On the next day re-boil the
syrup and fruit mixture,
remove from the heat and set
aside again for 24 hours.
Repeat this process until the
fruit and syrup have been
boiled a total of seven times.
Drain off the resulting cold
syrup and use to brush cake
bases or as a stock syrup for
fondant and glacé icing
reduction.

3 Place the pineapple rings on
a wire rack until dry
enough to handle, when they
should be stored between
sheets of waxed paper ready for
use. The candied pineapple
may be cut into small wedge-
shaped segments and placed in
an attractive gift box lined with
waxed paper to prevent the
fruit sticking. Candied
pineapple makes an ideal gift
for someone to use as
confectionery decorations or
just simply to eat and enjoy!

CARAMEL GLAZED FRUITS

Ingredients
a selection of fruits:
    cherries
    green and black grapes
    firm, just ripe strawberries
    mandarins
225g (8oz) granulated
    (superfine) sugar, warmed
60ml (4 tbsp) water
pinch of cream of tartar

1 Wash the cherries and
grapes, leave to drain and
dry on absorbent kitchen
paper. Check over the
strawberries for any blemished
fruit, carefully wiping with a
clean moist cloth and leaving
the stalks on the berries. Peel
the mandarins and separate the
segments.

2 Make the glaze by placing
the warmed sugar and water
in a heavy-based saucepan and
warming over a low heat until
dissolved. Add the cream of
tartar and boil the mixture. Use
a pastry brush dipped into cold
water to brush down the inside
of the pan frequently to
prevent crystallization. Do not
stir the mixture. Continue
boiling until the caramel
becomes a very light golden
colour when it is ready for use.
Remove from the heat.

3 Dip the prepared fruit in
the caramel, either holding
the fruit by the stalk or picking
it up with a wooden cocktail
stick (toothpick). Place the
dipped fruits on a lightly
greased baking tray and leave
until set. Present in small paper
cases. Serve the fruits within
3–4 hours.

CRYSTALLIZED FLOWERS

Ingredients
1 fresh rose
small bunch of fresh violets
2–3 stems of fresh freesias
gum arabic
colourless spirit such as gin or
    vodka
caster (superfine) sugar

1 Ideally use flowers from your garden or a friend's garden rather than commercially grown flowers that may have been sprayed with insecticides. Check that the flowers are clean and then carefully remove the petals, placing these on a piece of absorbent kitchen paper. Discard any petals that are in any way damaged or blemished.

Prepare a solution of gum arabic dissolved in a little colourless spirit and also a small dish or tray of caster sugar.

2 Using a clean paint brush or small pastry brush, brush each petal with the gum arabic solution and then lay on the caster sugar. Sprinkle sugar lightly over each petal – try if possible not to bruise the petals but ensure they are fully coated with sugar.

Place the sugared petals on a wire rack to allow air to circulate around them so that they dry quicker.

3 When dry, carefully remove from the wire rack and use as required to decorate sweets and treats such as Cherry Whirls (*see page 32*) or for your favourite soufflé, cheesecake or sherry trifle. If the petals are to be stored for later use, keep them in an air-tight jar. An attractive box filled with crystallized petals would make a welcome gift for an enthusiastic cook or sugarcraft artist for them to use on their own creations.

A different and less expensive way of crystallizing petals is to use egg white instead of the gum arabic solution. The petals will not, however, dry ready for use as quickly as the ones treated with spirit which evaporates quite rapidly.

QUICK DECORATED CHOCOLATES

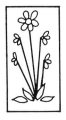   

This is a novel way to personalize a box of commercially made chocolates. You could of course use your own home-made chocolates.

Ingredients
box of assorted chocolates
royal icing
assorted paste food colourings
pouring fondant

1 Remove the chocolates from the box and sort into similar shapes.

Using assorted paste food colourings, mix various bright colours of royal icing. Half-fill greaseproof paper piping bags with the different icings, using a No1 or No0 nozzle. To help to make the royal icing stick to the chocolate a little better and avoid the risk of it flaking off, add a small amount of slightly warmed pouring fondant to the royal icing.

2 Using the patterns provided, pipe the floral motifs and stems and leaves on to the chocolates.

Names can also be piped on with very tiny lettering.

3 Place the finished chocolates in paper or foil cases.

Instead of replacing the chocolates in their original box, use an attractive gift box with a ribbon and gift tag to make a really special individual present.

CHOCOLATE LIQUEURS

Ingredients
prepared milk or plain
  chocolate cases (*see page 12*)
225g (8oz) granulated sugar
60ml (4 tbsp) cold water
30ml (2 tbsp) liqueur or spirit
melted plain or milk chocolate
  (*see page 10*)

1 Choose a selection of
attractive shapes of
chocolate cases, preferably
deep-moulded for the best
results.

2 Next make the liqueur
syrup. Place the sugar and
water in a small heavy-based
saucepan and bring to the boil
over a high heat to dissolve the
sugar. Boil the syrup to 108°C
(225°F) – transparent icing on
a sugar thermometer. Use a
pastry brush dipped in cold
water to brush down the inside
of the pan frequently to
prevent crystallization.

Pour the mixture into a
measuring jug and stand this in
tepid water. Add ice cubes to
the water to bring down the
temperature. Add the liqueur
or spirit and shake gently to
mix. The syrup is ready to use
when cold.

Using a small cream or milk
jug, pour the syrup into the
moulds leaving a small space at
the top of each so that a thin
film of chocolate can be
applied to seal the liqueur.
Leave in a cool place (not a
refrigerator) for 24 hours to
allow the surface to crystallize.

3 Using a small palette knife,
gently smooth a small
amount of melted chocolate
over the surface of each
chocolate liqueur to seal the
syrup. Leave to set.

Everyone needs to be
warned before eating a
chocolate with a liquid filling,
so carefully wrap each variety
in different coloured foil which
will also serve to identify the
flavours easily. Pack in a sturdy
gift box to avoid damaging the
fragile chocolates.
NOTE   If using a liqueur with a
high sugar content, you will
need to reduce the amount of
sugar in the recipe – otherwise
the syrup will crystallize too
quickly. Do not be tempted to
add more than the amount of
liqueur given in the recipe.

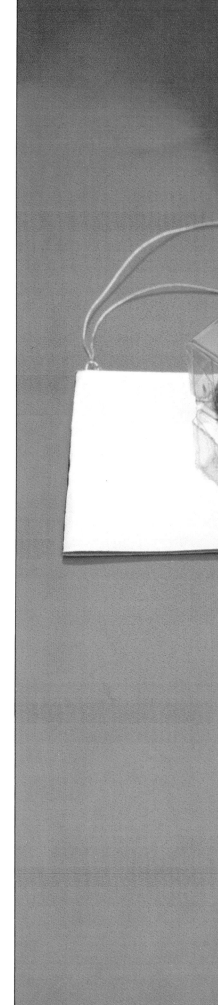

CHERRY WHIRLS

Ingredients

225g (8oz) cocktail cherries in maraschino, or glacé cherries and maraschino liqueur

melted plain or milk chocolate (*see page 10*)

crystallized rose petals (*see page 27*)

1 If you decide to make your own liqueur-soaked fruit rather than buy cocktail cherries, prepare the fruit a few days in advance to allow the flavour to penetrate. Place the glacé cherries (leave the coating syrup on) in a screw-topped jar or plastic container with air-tight lid and pour over the maraschino liqueur. Leave the fruit to marinate gently, shaking the container occasionally to mix. Drain the liqueur from the fruit and stand the cherries on a piece of absorbent kitchen paper ready for use.

2 Prepare small chocolate drops by piping melted chocolate on to waxed paper with a greaseproof piping bag.

When the drops are partly set, place a liqueur-soaked cherry on each – the chocolate should hold the cherry in place when fully set.

3 Turn the remaining chocolate left after preparation of the centres into piping or thickened chocolate. Stir a few drops of cold water into the chocolate, carefully mixing after each drop. The chocolate will gradually become thicker making it ideal for piping through a nozzle and retaining its shape.

Place a No42 nozzle in a greaseproof paper piping bag and three-quarters fill with the thickened chocolate. Pipe a whirl of chocolate over each cherry centre, starting at the base and winding round to the top. Take care to cover the whole cherry with chocolate to seal it completely.

While the chocolate is still soft, place a tiny piece of crystallized rose petal on each whirl to give a simple, classic finish to the chocolate. Place the finished chocolates in paper cases.

PINEAPPLE KIRSCH CREAMS

Ingredients
25ml (5 tsp) double (thick)
   dairy cream
90g (3oz) white chocolate,
   chopped
kirsch to taste
glacé pineapple (*see page 24*)
24 prepared white chocolate
   cases (*see page 10*)
melted white chocolate (*see page
   10*)
crystallized violets (*see page 27*)

1 Bring the cream to the boil
   in a saucepan. Remove from
the heat and add the chopped
chocolate. Continue stirring
until it has all melted and there
are no lumps. Stir in some
kirsch to taste and leave the
mixture to cool.
   Cut the glacé pineapple into
small pieces and place two or
three in each prepared case.

2 Fill a greaseproof paper
   piping bag with the cool
but not firm kirsch-flavoured
white ganache mixture. The
mixture should still be runny.
If the mixture has become too
firm, warm it gently over a
bowl of hot water, stirring
continuously. Pipe the mixture
into the white chocolate cases,
leaving just enough space to
smooth off the base. When
piping in the mixture, pipe into
all the spaces around the glacé
pineapple so that it becomes
completely sealed. Leave until
firm.

3 Using a little melted white
   chocolate and a small
palette knife, smooth off the
base of each piece. Leave to
set, then turn out the finished
chocolates from the moulds.
Decorate with small pieces of
crystallized violet.

CHERRY BRANDY CUPS

Ingredients
12 glacé cherries
brandy
25ml (5 tsp) double (thick)
  dairy cream
90g (3oz) milk chocolate,
  chopped
24 prepared plain chocolate
  cases (*see page 12*)
melted plain chocolate (*see page
  10*)

1 Place the cherries in a
screw-topped jar or air-
tight plastic container, pour the
brandy over the fruit and leave
to stand for about 12 hours,
gently shaking the container
occasionally.

2 Prepare the ganache filling.
Bring the cream to the boil
in a saucepan. Remove from
the heat and add the chopped
chocolate. Continue stirring
until it has all melted and there
are no lumps. Add some
brandy to taste and stir in
thoroughly. Leave the mixture
to cool.

3 Drain the juice from the
cherries and stand them on
absorbent kitchen paper. Cut
each cherry in half and place a
half in each of the prepared
chocolate cases. If you place
the cherries in the cases with
the rounded side facing
downwards, they will fit better
and be easier to finish.

4 Fill a greaseproof paper
piping bag with the cooled
but not firm ganache mixture.
The mixture should be runny;
if it has set too firmly, simply
warm it over a bowl of hot
water stirring constantly until
the correct consistency is
obtained.

Pipe the ganache mixture
into the chocolate cases filling
in the spaces around the
cherries to seal them and
stopping just short of the top,
thus enabling a thin coat of
chocolate to be applied. Leave
the ganache to become firm.

5 Using a small palette knife,
smooth off the base of each
chocolate with some melted
chocolate. Leave to set. Then
remove the chocolates from the
moulds and place in paper
cases ready for presentation.

6 Decorate the tops of the
chocolates with red and
green royal icing to make a
cherry and leaf motif.

COFFEE AND WALNUT SUPREMES

Ingredients
45ml (3 tbsp) double (thick) dairy cream
10ml (2 tsp) instant coffee granules
175g (6oz) plain or milk chocolate, chopped
melted plain or milk chocolate for dipping (*see page 10*)
even-sized walnut pieces

1 Make the chocolate centres first. Bring the cream to the boil in a saucepan, add the coffee granules and stir to dissolve. Remove from the heat and add the chopped chocolate. Continue stirring until it has all melted and there are no lumps.

Pour the mixture into a foil-lined baking tray or special sweet-making tray (*see page 12*). To obtain the required depth of filling using the recipe given, the tray should measure about 10 × 17.5-cm (4 × 7-in). Leave the mixture to cool and set fully, refrigerating if necessary to quicken the setting time.

2 When fully set, turn the slab of mixture out of the tray and trim all the edges with a knife that has been dipped in hot water and dried. Cut the slab into pieces about 12-mm × 2.5-cm ($\frac{1}{2}$ × 1-in). Place the cut shapes on waxed paper ready for dipping.

3 Using a dipping fork, dip each centre into the melted chocolate, allowing the excess to drain away. Smooth the base of the centre along the edge of the chocolate pan or use a palette knife. Place the chocolates on waxed paper to set. If 'feet' start to form because too much chocolate was left on the centres, carefully slide each one along the waxed paper, leaving behind the excess chocolate.

Before the chocolate sets fully, decorate each Supreme with a neat piece of walnut.

SPECIAL TRUFFLES

Ingredients
45ml (3 tbsp) double (thick)
dairy cream
175g (6oz) milk, plain or white
chocolate, chopped
30ml (2 tbsp) brandy for milk
chocolate, or rum for plain
chocolate, or kirsch or
Champagne for white
chocolate
icing (confectioner's) sugar for
dusting
melted milk, plain or white
chocolate for dipping (*see
page 10*)

1 First make the filling for the
centres. Bring the cream to
the boil in a saucepan. Remove
from the heat and add the
chopped chocolate. Continue
stirring until it has all melted
and there are no lumps. Stir in
the appropriate alcoholic
flavouring and mix thoroughly.
Pour the mixture into a
shallow tray or plastic bowl
and leave aside to cool
completely. To quicken the
process, you can chill the
mixture in a refrigerator.

2 When the mixture is
completely cool and firm,
turn it out on to a work
surface lightly dusted with
icing sugar. Flatten the mixture
using a rolling pin and your
hands to make a pliable,
plastic-type paste.
   Roll the mixture into long
sausage shapes, again using a
little icing sugar. Cut into
even-sized pieces as required.
   Roll each portion lightly into
a neat ball shape. The warmth
from your hands will at this
stage melt the chocolate a little.
Place each rolled ball on waxed
paper. The truffles could be
rolled in chocolate vermicelli to
make an attractive finish.

3 Using a dipping fork or
skewer, dip each truffle into
the melted chocolate (of the
same type used for the centres),
allowing any excess to drain
away. Place the dipped centres
on a wire rack and as the
chocolate coating sets, roll the
truffle along the wire rack to
make a peaked textured finish
as shown. Leave to set.
   If the truffle centres are not
completely covered with the
first dipping, repeat the
process. Place the finished
truffles in paper cases ready for
presentation.

ALPINE BRANDY LOG

Ingredients

175g (6oz) milk chocolate, chopped
45ml (3 tbsp) double (thick) dairy cream
30ml (2 tbsp) brandy
green-coloured marzipan
melted milk chocolate (*see page 10*)
icing (confectioner's) sugar

1 First prepare the ganache filling. Bring the cream to the boil in a saucepan. Remove from the heat and add the chopped chocolate. Continue stirring until it has all melted and there are no lumps. Add the brandy and stir in thoroughly. Pour the mixture into a shallow tray or plastic bowl. Leave to cool and set.

Roll out the green-coloured marzipan into a long narrow strip, using a little icing sugar for dusting.

Turn the ganache filling out of the container and make into a pliable, plastic-type mixture. Use a rolling pin and a little icing sugar dusting to soften the paste slightly. Roll out long sausage shapes and place along the edge of the green-coloured marzipan strip.

Wrap the green-coloured marzipan around the chocolate centre, trim off any excess marzipan and re-roll the log to neaten the shape.

3 Place the log on a sheet of waxed paper and brush melted chocolate along the length, using a pastry brush, or texture the surface with a fork while still soft. Leave to set.

Cut the log into small pieces using a sharp knife dipped into hot water. Lightly dust the surface of each piece with icing sugar and then place in paper cases ready for packing.

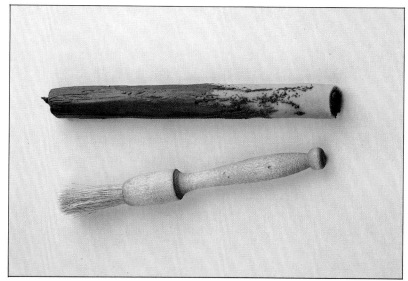

GINGER CHRISTMAS TREE DECORATIONS

Ingredients
150g (5oz) butter
225g (8oz) plain (all-purpose)
  flour
125g (4oz) brown sugar
7g ($\frac{1}{4}$oz) ground ginger
pinch of baking powder
150g (5oz) golden syrup,
  slightly warmed
melted plain or milk chocolate
  (*see page 10*)
sugarpaste
marzipan
royal icing
assorted paste food colourings
  or food colour pens
egg white

Rub the butter through the dry ingredients to make a fine crumble. Add the syrup and mix to a smooth dough. Leave in the refrigerator for about 1 hour before using.

Roll out the biscuit dough to about 9mm (⅜-in) thickness, dusting with a little flour. Cut out round and oval shapes with food cutters. Make a small hole with a No4 nozzle in each shape for the hanger. Place the biscuits on a lightly greased baking tray and bake at 190°C (370°F) Gas Mark 5 for about 12 minutes or until golden. Leave on the trays until firm to the touch but not completely cold, then transfer to a wire rack and leave to finish cooling.

When cool spread the base of each biscuit with melted milk or plain chocolate and leave on waxed paper until quite set.

Colour some marzipan or sugarpaste in a variety of different colours and use to make various cut-out Christmas faces such as Santa, snowmen and angels. Attach the shapes to the biscuits with a little melted chocolate or royal icing. Pipe the eyes on with white and brown-coloured royal icing.

Alternatively, the biscuits can be decorated with painted Christmas scenes – these are more suitable as gifts for adults. Roll out some sugarpaste thinly and cut to the required shape. Spread a thin layer of royal icing on each biscuit and attach a sugarpaste cut-out. Leave for a few hours to become firm.

Use edible food colourings and a fine paint brush or edible food colour pens to paint your favourite Christmas scenes. Many ideas can be gleaned from gift wrapping paper and Christmas cards.

When the biscuits are decorated, you can thread some gold or silver gift tie through the hole in each one to enable you to hang them on your Christmas tree.

FLORENTINES

Ingredients
50g (2oz) butter
50g (2oz) brown sugar
5ml (1 tsp) honey
15ml (1 tbsp) chopped walnuts
15ml (1 tbsp) nibbed or
  chopped flaked almonds
15ml (1 tbsp) chopped glacé
  cherries
5ml (1 tsp) chopped glacé
  ginger
5ml (1 tsp) evaporated milk
5ml (1 tsp) plain (all-purpose)
  flour
melted milk, plain or white
  chocolate (*see page 10*)

1 Melt the butter in a
  saucepan, add the sugar and
honey and bring to the boil.
Remove from the heat.

Stir in the prepared nuts,
cherries and ginger, then add
the evaporated milk and lastly
the flour. Lightly grease a
miniature bun tin (pan) with
butter or margarine. Using a
teaspoon, place small amounts
of the florentine mixture in
each indent. Bake the
florentines at 190°C (375°F)
Gas Mark 5 for 8–9 minutes or
until golden brown.

Leave the florentines in the
bun tin for a short time until
they start to set and become
firm. You can neaten the edges
with a small knife while the
caramel is setting. When
slightly cool, remove the
florentines from the tin, using
a small knife to release them,
and place on waxed paper
ready for decoration. If you
should leave the florentines in
the tin too long and they stick,
just warm them slightly in the
oven to release them.

2 Spread some melted
  chocolate on waxed paper,
smoothing out with a cranked
palette knife. Shake the paper a
little to assist the flow of the
chocolate and to obtain a flat
surface. Leave to set.

Pour some more melted
chocolate over the previously
prepared chocolate and while
still soft, use a comb scraper to
create a wavy pattern on the
chocolate. Move the scraper
from side to side along the
chocolate in a smooth flowing
action. Leave to set.

3 Using a small round food
  cutter the same diameter as
the florentines, cut out a
matching number of discs of
chocolate. Brush a little melted
chocolate on the flat side of
each florentine and attach the
prepared discs. You can spread
and texture the chocolate
directly on to the florentine but
the recommended way is far
easier and looks neater when
finished.

Package a selection of milk,
plain and white chocolate
decorated florentines – they
make a welcome gift or a super
tea-time treat!

CAKE TRUFFLES

Ingredients

275g (10oz) plain or chocolate
    cake crumbs
50g (2oz) ground almonds
25g (1oz) apricot jam
60ml (4 tbsp) evaporated milk
50–90g (2–3oz) plain chocolate,
    melted
icing (confectioner's) sugar for
    dusting
melted plain and milk chocolate
    for dipping (*see page 10*)
plain and milk chocolate
    vermicelli
chocolate shavings
roasted flaked almonds
cocoa powder

1 Mix the cake crumbs and
ground almonds together
and then add the jam,
evaporated milk and chocolate,
mixing thoroughly to a firm
paste. The amount of chocolate
required depends upon the
moisture content of your cake
crumbs. Chill for 30 minutes
before use.

2 Roll the mixture out into a
long sausage shape and cut
into small pieces. Roll half of
the pieces into neat round balls
and the other half into small
finger shapes. Use a little icing
sugar for dusting to prevent
the mixture from sticking to
the work surface.

3 Prepare your work area so
that the finishing off runs in
a smooth logical sequence.
Have ready your prepared
truffle centres, the dipping
chocolate. followed by the
masking material and finally a
sheet of waxed paper to place
the finished truffles on. You
could even place the truffles
directly in the paper cases if
they do not require any further
decoration.

4 At this stage it is best to
have some assistance from
another person to roll the
chocolate-coated truffles in the
chosen masking material as
your hands will be covered
with melted chocolate. Take a
small amount of melted
chocolate in the palm of both
hands and roll each truffle
gently in your hands to cover
with a thin film of chocolate.

Place the coated truffle in the
masking material and ask your
helper to roll the truffle and
completely cover it in masking
material. The truffles are then
left on waxed paper to set
fully.

The truffles may be left as
they are or can be further
decorated by lightly dusting
with icing sugar, using a tea
strainer or very fine sieve. A
fine dusting of equal parts of
icing sugar and cocoa powder
mixed together makes a nice
finish on truffles that have just
been rolled in chocolate and
not actually masked. Place the
truffles in paper cases.

FANCY CAKES

Ingredients
apricot jam
fancy cakes baked in small bun
   tins (pans)
glacé icing
instant coffee granules
melted chocolate (*see page 10*)
assorted food colourings
buttercream
selection of decorations, nuts
   and glacé fruits

1 Boil the apricot jam in a saucepan (adding a little water to thin if necessary) and using a pastry brush, lightly brush the jam over the top of each cake to the edges. This not only seals the cake, therefore keeping it fresher for a longer period, but also adds another flavour.

2 Divide the cakes into six separate batches ready for the different colours of icing. Warm some white glacé icing over a pan of hot water and use to ice the tops of one batch. Use a small palette knife and take the icing to just short of the edges to allow for a little flow.
   Divide the remaining glacé icing and keep it warm over bowls or pans of hot water. Colour one half lemon and one half pink and use to ice the tops of two more batches. Then mix the two colours of glacé icing together to make pale orange, adding more orange food colouring if required. Ice another batch. For the last two batches add a little instant coffee dissolved in hot water and use to ice one batch. Then stir in some melted chocolate to make chocolate icing for the remaining cakes.

3 Using buttercream, pipe the designs as shown on the cakes and decorate as liked.

FRUITY CRUNCHIES

Ingredients

equal quantities of:
    chopped walnuts
    chopped hazelnuts
    flaked almonds
    sultanas
    glacé cherries
    cornflakes
melted white chocolate (*see page 10*)
melted plain chocolate (*see page 10*)

1 Set out some small paper cases ready for the mixture.

2 Place all the nuts and fruits in a large bowl and stand it over a pan of hot water. Add the cornflakes and sufficient melted white chocolate to bind all the ingredients to a dropping consistency.

    Using a teaspoon, pile small amounts of the mixture high in the paper cases, keeping the texture rough. Leave to set.

3 Use scissors to snip off the end of a small greaseproof paper piping bag filled with melted plain chocolate. With a short side-to-side movement spin some fine lines of chocolate over the crunchies. Leave to set.

LITTLE CHRISTMAS PUDDINGS

Ingredients
300g (10oz) plain or chocolate
    sponge cake crumbs
25g (1oz) ground almonds
25g (1oz) apricot jam
60ml (4 fl oz) evaporated milk
30ml (2 tbsp) rum
5ml (1 tsp) chopped walnuts
5ml (1 tsp) chopped glacé
    cherries
5ml (1 tsp) chopped glacé
    ginger
5ml (1 tsp) chopped sultanas
about 50g (2oz) melted
    chocolate (*see page 10*)
icing (confectioner's) sugar for
    dusting
natural marzipan or white
    sugarpaste
melted plain chocolate (*see page
    10*)
pouring fondant or glacé icing
egg-yellow paste food
    colouring
green-coloured royal icing
red-coloured royal icing

1 Mix the cake crumbs and
  ground almonds together,
then add the other ingredients
and mix well to a firm paste.
The amount of chocolate
required depends upon the
moisture content of your
sponge cake crumbs. Chill for
30 minutes before use.
   Roll the mixture into a long
sausage shape, using a little
icing sugar for dusting. Cut
into even-sized pieces, then roll
each one into a neat ball shape
and place on waxed paper.

2 Prepare the plates for the
  puddings by rolling out
some marzipan or sugarpaste
thinly and cutting out some
small fluted circles. Place the
circles in small bun tins (pans)
or plastic fruit trays to dry in a
curved shape.

3 Using a dipping fork or
  skewer, dip each centre into
the melted chocolate allowing
any excess to drain away. Place
each dipped ball on a prepared
plate. Leave to set.

4 Warm the pouring fondant
  or glacé icing in a double
jacketed pan and colour egg-
yellow. Using a small
greaseproof paper piping bag
with a small hole cut at one
end, pipe a little of the icing
on top of each pudding to
represent custard, allowing
some to run down the side.

5 Fit No2 nozzles in two
  small greaseproof paper
piping bags and half-fill with
green- and red-coloured royal
icing respectively. Pipe three
small 'spikes' for holly leaves
on each pudding and three red
berries.

CRISPY CHOIRBOYS

Ingredients

puffed rice cereal
melted milk or plain chocolate
 (*see page 10*)
marzipan
white sugarpaste or flower
 paste
red, flesh, egg-yellow, brown
 and black paste food
 colourings
royal icing
rice paper

1 Place the puffed rice cereal
 in a bowl over hot water
and mix in sufficient melted
chocolate to cover the cereal
and bind together.

 Lay a sheet of waxed paper
on a cake board and arrange 4-
cm (1¾-in) diameter food
cutters on top. Line each food
cutter with a narrow strip of
waxed paper.

2 To make the body shapes,
 fill the chocolate and cereal
mixture into the lined cutters
using a teaspoon. Flatten the
top smoothly with the back of
the spoon. Leave to set before
removing the shapes from the
cutters.

 Pipe some chocolate discs or
large drops on to waxed paper
and leave to set. Attach a
prepared body shape to each
disc with a little melted
chocolate, supporting if
necessary until set.

3 Colour some marzipan with
 red paste food colouring for
the arms and roll out into a
sausage shape. Cut to length
and attach to the body with a
little melted chocolate. Next
cut out a small fluted circle of
thinly rolled white sugarpaste
and attach, to form the ruffle.
Make a small depression for the
head in the centre of the ruffle
with a modelling tool or your
thumb.

 Roll a small oval shape in
flesh-coloured marzipan for the
head and indent the eyes with a
modelling tool or end of a
paint brush. Attach a tiny ball
of flesh-coloured marzipan for
the nose with egg white. Press
on a tiny ball of red-coloured
marzipan for the mouth, with
the end of a paint brush,
moving it up and down to
make a long oval mouth giving
the impression of a choirboy
reaching a high note. Attach
the head to the ruffle on the
body with white royal icing.

 Pipe the eyes with white
royal icing and a No2 nozzle
and overpipe with brown-
coloured royal icing. Pipe the
hair on with egg-yellow-,
brown- or black-coloured royal
icing using a No1 nozzle to
pull up spikes as shown. The
face can be tinted with petal
dust or sprayed with an
airbrush using pinky-orange
colour to create a complexion.

4 Cover the choirboys in
 cellophane tied with an
attractive ribbon and bow and
gift tag. Alternatively, present
them singly or in groups in
boxes. They also make original
party place settings especially
when further decorated with a
name or inscription plaque in
sugarpaste.

LOLLY FACES

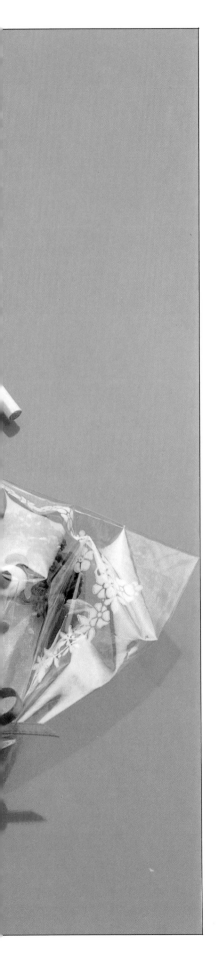

Ingredients
packet of assorted fruit-
    flavoured and toffee lollies
royal icing
marzipan
sugarpaste
egg white
assorted paste food colourings

1 Unwrap the lollies and press
the sticks into a block of
polystyrene foam to make
working on them easier.

2 You can be really creative
with these novelty faces so
colour the marzipan and
sugarpaste in bright attractive
colours that young children
will appreciate.
  Hats are easily made from
semi-circles, balls or strips of
marzipan as shown. Attach the
brims of the hats with a little
egg white and then decorate
them with badges or flowers.
  Miniature plaits of hair can
be formed from strips of
marzipan. You could also press
coloured marzipan through a
tea strainer or clay gun to
create a good effect. Attach the
hair to the lollies with a little
royal icing.
  Bow-ties are quick to make
from thinly rolled-out
sugarpaste cut into small
triangular shapes and attached
together with a tiny ball of
sugarpaste and some egg white.
Spotted bow ties are made by
pressing tiny balls of coloured
sugarpaste in the rolled-out
paste at the first stage.

3 Pipe eyes on the faces in
white royal icing with a
No2 nozzle, then overpipe with
brown. Noses, mouths and ears
are made from marzipan and
attached with tiny dabs of royal
icing.
  The finished lollies can be
wrapped in cellophane and tied
with an attractive bow and gift
tag.

SHORTBREAD SETTINGS

Ingredients
packet of round shortbread
  biscuits
melted chocolate (*see page 10*)
sugarpaste
marzipan (optional)
icing (confectioner's) sugar for
  dusting
flower paste (optional)
assorted paste food colourings
royal icing
non-pareils

1 Spread the back of each
shortbread biscuit with
melted chocolate. This gives
them more stability for
handling and also introduces
another texture and delicious
flavour. Place the biscuits on
waxed paper and leave to set.

2 Colour some sugarpaste or
marzipan and roll out quite
thinly, using a little icing sugar
for dusting. Using a fluted
cutter the size of the biscuit cut
out a disc for each biscuit.

Attach the sugarpaste or
marzipan discs to the biscuits
with royal icing. Leave to set.

3 Roll out some sugarpaste
(or use flower paste) of a
different colour thinly. Using
plunger or flower cutters,
stamp out flower shapes. Place
on clean foam sponge, pressing
lightly in the centre to make a
depression. Leave to set. Also
cut out some green-coloured
leaves.

Pipe a bulb of royal icing in
the centre of each flower and
lightly press into coloured non-
pareils.

Attach the flowers and
leaves to the prepared biscuit
bases, using a little royal icing.
To complete the place settings,
pipe the guest's name in
coloured royal icing, using a
No1 nozzle.

PRESENTATION AND PACKAGING

After spending a considerable time producing your delicious hand-made sweets and treats, it is worthwhile devoting just as much thought to their packaging and presentation. Give your sweets and treats that individual look, that personalized touch, that extra special something!

Beautifully presented home-made sweets make ideal gifts, showing you care enough about the recipients to spend time creating attractive packaging.

You can buy small gift boxes, gift tags and novelty bags from stationers, sugarcraft suppliers and greeting card shops. Paper and foil cases can also be purchased from the same places.

Truffles (*see page 41*) can be packed in a gift box and decorated with a shiny ribbon and bow – add a special touch with some tiny silk flowers.

A transparent heart-shaped box decorated with a miniature bouquet of flowers is ideal for Valentine's Day, engagement or wedding receptions as take-home gifts for the guests.

Make your own chocolate box, using a commercially available mould. Pipe a decorative edging in royal icing and pack your chocolates inside.

Small paper or foil gift bags look wonderful packed with Fruity Crunchies (*see page 52*) or Truffles (*see page 41*). Tie with a matching ribbon, bow and gift tag.

Keep the contents a surprise, pack the chocolates inside and tie with a ribbon and bow. Edible flowers make an extra special feature.

Cover half a cabbage with decorative foil gift wrapping paper and stick lots of Lolly Faces (*see page 58*) into it to make a super table centrepiece for a children's tea party.

Tiny boxes which hold one or two small chocolates (*see page 41*) or truffles (*see page 41*) make attractive party place settings or take-home gifts – or can even be used as Christmas tree decorations.

PIPED CHOCOLATE DECORATIONS

Ingredients

melted milk, plain or white
 chocolate (*see page 10*)
water or glycerine

1 Prepare templates of the designs to be used. Trace the patterns provided on to white cartridge paper. Also cut out small sheets of waxed paper the same size as the templates.

2 Prepare the melted chocolate for piping. For this purpose you need to thicken the chocolate. Add a few drops of water or glycerine, stirring gently after each addition. After a few additions the chocolate will start to thicken, do not add *too much* liquid as this would make the chocolate too thick for piping. Keep the chocolate over a bowl of warm water.

Half-fill a small greaseproof paper piping bag with the chocolate mixture and use scissors to cut a neat hole at the end of the bag about the size of a No2 nozzle.

3 Place pieces of waxed paper over the templates and pipe as for royal icing, following the outlines carefully and neatly. Avoid shaking the paper, as this will make the chocolate run. Place the piped pieces on a cake board to finish setting, which does not take long.

4 Small crystallized petals or coloured dragees make interesting alternative finishes. Peel the piped shapes off the waxed paper and store ready to use between sheets of waxed paper. Alternatively, you can pack the shapes in gift boxes to give to your friends. Piped chocolate shapes make lovely decorations for special desserts, ice creams, soufflés, cheesecakes and many small cakes and gâteaux.

Examples of piped chocolate decorations